George Washington Carver

A Photo-Illustrated Biography
by Margo McLoone

Reading Consultant:
Dr. Gail Lowe
Anacostia Museum

Bridgestone Books
an Imprint of Capstone Press

Facts about George Washington Carver

- George Washington Carver was a scientist and a teacher.
- He was an award-winning painter.
- He was a member of England's Royal Society of Arts.
- He is in the National Inventors Hall of Fame.

Bridgestone Books are published by Capstone Press
151 Good Counsel Drive, P.O. Box 669, Mankato, Minnesota 56002
http://www.capstone-press.com

Library of Congress Cataloging-in-Publication Data
McLoone, Margo.
   George Washington Carver/by Margo McLoone.
   p. cm.--(Read and discover photo-illustrated biographies)
   Includes bibliographical references and index.
   Summary: A brief biography of the African American scientist who overcame tremendous
   hardship to make unusual and important discoveries in the field of agriculture.
   ISBN 1-56065-516-X
1. Carver, George Washington, 1864?-1943--Juvenile literature. 2. Afro-American
agriculturists--Biography--Juvenile literature. 3. Agriculturists--United States--Biography--
Juvenile literature. 4. Afro-Americans--Biography--Juvenile literature. [1. Carver, George
Washington, 1864?-1943. 2. Agriculturists. 3. Afro-Americans--Biography.]
   I. Title. II. Series.
S417.C3M299 1997
630'.92--dc21
[B]
                                      96-37414
                                         CIP
                                           AC

Photo credits
Schomburg Center, cover, 12, 18
Unicorn/Andre Jenny, 6; Martha McBride, 10
Bettmann, 4, 8, 14, 16, 20

  3 4 5 6 04 03 02 01

Table of Contents

Plant Wizard 5

Young Orphan 7

Student of Nature 9

First Jobs 11

College Education 13

Teacher at Tuskegee 15

Friend to Farmers 17

The Peanut Man 19

International Fame 21

Words from George Washington Carver 22

Important Dates in George Washington Carver's Life . 23

Words to Know 23

Read More 24

Useful Addresses 24

Internet Sites 24

Index 24

Plant Wizard

George Washington Carver was a creative scientist. He studied and did experiments with plants. An experiment is a scientific test.

George is best known for his work with peanuts. He made more than 300 products from peanuts. Some of these products were ink, milk, and soap.

George was a student and a teacher of botany. Botany is the study of plants. He spent most of his life teaching at Tuskegee Institute in Tuskegee, Alabama. He taught botany to nonwhite students.

George also taught farmers how to grow healthy crops. Crops are plants grown for food. George wrote newsletters explaining how to plant, grow, and use crops.

George studied and taught botany, which is the science of plants.

BIRTHPLACE SITE

8

Young Orphan

George Carver was born on a farm near Diamond Grove, Missouri. He was born a slave. A slave is a person who is owned by someone else. George belonged to the Carver family. They owned slaves even though they did not like slavery.

The Carvers came from Germany and started a farm in Missouri. They could not find workers for their farm. So they bought an African-American woman named Mary. She gave birth to two sons. They were named Jim and George.

When George was a baby, he and his mother were stolen. The kidnappers planned to sell them in the southern states. The Carvers found George and brought him back to their farm. But George's mother was never seen again.

George was born on a farm near Diamond Grove, Missouri.

Student of Nature

George often wandered around the farm by himself. He looked at plants, collected rocks, and watched insects.

He became curious about life and color in nature. George liked flowers. Farmers in his area did not bother to plant flowers. They were too busy with crops. He secretly planted a flower garden near the woods. He began to paint pictures of his flowers.

George wanted to learn more about nature. He wanted to read and write. The Carvers sent him to school in Diamond Grove. He was turned away because he was African American. The Carvers sent George to a private teacher instead. George learned everything the tutor could teach him about science.

George liked flowers and was always curious about nature.

First Jobs

In 1877, George left the Carver farm. He went to live with a young couple. He attended a school for African Americans. Once again, he learned all he could.

George worked and traveled for 10 years. He had many jobs. He worked as a cook and a janitor. He started his own laundry business.

George met many people. He wrote and received a lot of letters. Once, he learned that his mail had been sent to another person named George Carver. George added a W to his name. People said that the W must stand for Washington. He became known as George Washington Carver.

George left the Carver farm in 1877. He worked on a farm similar to this one near Diamond Grove, Missouri.

College Education

George wanted to go to college. He applied by mail to Highland College in Kansas. He was accepted. But when he arrived, he was turned away. African Americans were not allowed to attend.

In 1890, George attended Simpson College in Iowa. His favorite subject was art. His art teacher, Etta Budd, liked his paintings of plants. But she wanted him to study botany. She thought he could make a better living in science than in art.

Etta told George to go to Iowa State College in Ames, Iowa. He decided to go. Now he could learn all about plants.

George graduated from Iowa State in 1894. He stayed to teach and to run the school's farm.

George attended Iowa State College where he studied botany.

Teacher at Tuskegee

In 1896, George earned a master's degree in science. A master's degree is a degree awarded for study after college. George took a teaching job at the Tuskegee Institute in Alabama. He also wanted to educate African-American students. He wanted to help poor farmers.

George wanted his students to learn by seeing and doing. He took them on nature hikes. He helped them set up scientific experiments.

George called the students his children. Students thought he was a caring teacher.

George wanted his students to learn by seeing and doing.

Friend to Farmers

George liked helping farmers who lived near Tuskegee. He showed them how to keep the soil healthy. He taught them to make compost from weeds, feathers, and old clothing. Compost is a mixture that keeps the soil rich. He told them how to plant different crops to save the soil.

George told farmers to plant vegetable gardens for fresh, cheap food. He wrote articles about farming. These articles helped farmers grow, prepare, use, and save crops.

In 1904, George created a school on wheels. He made a wagon with dairy and crop displays. He went to different farms and taught the science of farming.

George liked to teach farmers how to keep their soil rich.

The Peanut Man

In 1921, George went to Washington, D.C. He spoke to members of Congress about peanuts. He talked about the value of peanuts for farmers. He wanted Congress to pass a law. The law would protect peanut sales in the United States.

George won support from Congress. He showed them more than 100 uses for peanuts. He created shampoo, dye, glue, medicine, candy, and ink. A dye changes the color of things.

George told why he was interested in peanuts. He wanted to understand the little secrets of nature. The peanut was just the right size for him.

George showed members of Congress more than 100 uses for peanuts.

International Fame

George was known all over the world. He created several products from peanuts and sweet potatoes. He developed rare dyes from soil.

George received many awards. He was honored for his creative science. People said he could have been rich and famous. But he was happy being useful and helpful to others.

On January 5, 1943, George died at Tuskegee. He was almost 80 years old.

In 1951, the George Washington Carver National Monument was built. It is on the 200-acre (80-hectare) farm where he was born.

George received many awards for his creativity in science.

Words from George Washington Carver

"To those who have not yet learned the secret of true happiness, begin now to study the little things in your own door yard."

Carver's advice to his students at Tuskegee Institute, 1897.

"God gave them [ideas for inventions] to me, how can I sell them to someone else?"

Carver's answer to a question at an interview in 1921. George was asked why he had not patented his inventions.

Important Dates in George Washington Carver's Life

1865—Born in Diamond Grove, Missouri

1894—Graduates from Iowa State College

1896—Earns a master of science degree

1896—Begins teaching at Tuskegee Institute in Alabama

1921—Speaks to U.S. Congress about the peanut industry

1923—Awarded Spingarn Medal (NAACP) for science

1928—Receives first of three honorary doctor of science degrees from Simpson College, Iowa; the others were from the University of Rochester, 1941, and Selma University, 1942

1935—Works for the U.S. Department of Agriculture

1938—A Hollywood movie is made about his life

1939—Receives the Franklin Delano Roosevelt Medal for science

1941—The George Washington Carver Foundation opens at Tuskegee

1943—Dies at Tuskegee Institute

Words to Know

botany (BOT-uh-nee)—the study of plants

compost (KOM-pohst)—a mixture that keeps soil rich

master's degree (MA-sterz DA-gree)—a degree awarded for continued study after college

scientific experiment (sye-uhn-TIF-ik ek-SPER-uh-ment)—a test a scientist does to learn about something

slave (SLAYV)—a person who is owned by someone else

Read More

Carey, Charles W. *George Washington Carver.* Journey To Freedom. Chanhassen, Minn.: Child's World, 1999.

Riley, John. *George Washington Carver: A Photo Biography.* Greensboro, N.C.: First Biographies, 2000.

Wellman, Sam. *George Washington Carver.* Heroes of the Faith. Philadelphia: Chelsea House Publishers, 1998.

Useful Addresses and Internet Sites

**The George Washington
  Carver Museum**
P.O. Drawer #10
Tuskegee, AL 36088

**George Washington
  Carver National Monument**
5646 Carver Road
Diamond, MO 64840

Africana.com: George Washington Carver
http://www.africana.com/tt_080.htm
World Book: George Washington Carver
http://www.worldbook.com/fun/aajourny/html/bh067.html

Index

botany, 5, 13
Budd, Etta, 13
compost, 17
crops, 5, 17
Diamond Grove,
   Missouri, 7, 9

experiment, 5, 15
Germany, 7
Highland College, 13
Iowa State College, 13
master's degree, 15

peanut, 5, 19, 21
slave, 7, 9
Tuskegee Institute, 5,
   15, 21
Washington, D.C., 19